Ian Brownhill is a barrister at 39 Essex Chambers, the Assistant Coroner for Kent and a Recorder sitting in the Family Court. Ian has practiced in the Court of Protection for over a decade and was awarded the Legal 500 Bar Awards junior of the year for Court of Protection and community care in 2023. Outside of court work, Ian trains and lectures in respect of adult safeguarding and mental capacity, he teaches on the Best Interests Assessor Course at the University of Central Lancashire.

Ian has appeared in many of the most important recent judgments in respect of mental capacity, this included the decision in *JB* which was heard in the Supreme Court. In respect of cases involving high net worth individuals, Ian regularly advises deputies and public bodies in this regard. He appeared in the *Hinduja* litigation and for the applicant in *Re BU* in respect of predatory marriage.

An Introduction to Health and Welfare Disputes involving High Net Worth Individuals

An Introduction to Health and Welfare Disputes involving High Net Worth Individuals

Ian Brownhill

Barrister, Lincoln's Inn

Recorder of the Family Court and
His Majesty's Assistant Coroner for Kent

Law Brief Publishing

Published 2025 by Law Brief Publishing, an imprint of Law Brief Publishing Ltd
30 The Parks
Minehead
Somerset
TA24 8BT

www.lawbriefpublishing.com

Paperback: 978-1-916698-85-7

This book is dedicated to all the professionals who spend their working lives promoting the best interests of people who lack the mental capacity to make their own decisions.

PREFACE

There is a common misconception in Court of Protection proceedings that property and affairs cases before the court are in respect of the wealthy, whilst health and welfare cases focus on the health and welfare decisions of individuals of lower socio-economic status. This perception causes a bias (conscious or otherwise) in processes operated by statutory services and creates misapprehension as to the powers and responsibilities of those making decisions on behalf of those individuals who do not rely on care, support or treatment which is funded by the state.

This book cannot be a compendious guide to every dispute as to health and welfare matters which impact on high net worth individuals who lack the mental capacity to make certain decisions for themselves. Rather, it is intended to be a prompt for social workers, health professionals, professional deputies, case managers and private client lawyers when grappling with these issues.

I remain grateful to my instructing solicitors, the Official Solicitor, the Public Guardian and others who seek my advice and representation in respect of these matters both inside and outside of court.

The law is, to the best of my ability, correct as of 16 December 2024.

Ian Brownhill
39 Essex Chambers

CONTENTS

CONTENTS

CHAPTER ONE

INTRODUCTION

The term high net worth is ubiquitous. It has appeared as a term in a small number[1] of Court of Protection judgments. HMRC have defined the term in different ways in recent years, at the time of writing, it is understood that their High Net Worth Unit deals with the tax affairs of individual taxpayers with a net worth of more than £10 million. Elsewhere, the Financial Conduct Authority operates a different definition.

Some would consider those individuals who are not eligible for state funded care and support to be wealthy. It would be artificial for this book to attempt to identify a threshold as to when an individual would be considered to be high net worth; the Mental Capacity Act 2005 and the Court of Protection does not make such a distinction.

Rather, this book considers health and welfare issues which present when wealthier individuals lose the mental capacity to make certain decisions for themselves. This book is not a replacement for legal advice which is tailored to a particular case, rather it is a starting point to thinking about these issues.

As this book was being drafted, the Law Commission were reviewing the law in respect of revocation of wills upon marriage due to concerns as to predatory marriage. Sadly, this book was drafted shortly following the death of the Honourable Mrs Justice Roberts DBE who had presided over the case of *Re BU* [2021] EWCOP 54. That

---

1 *Re JMA* [2018] EWCOP 19; *Re H* [2015] EWCOP 52; *XZ v The Public Guardian* [2015] EWCOP 35;

complicated case concerned questions as to mental capacity, undue influence and coercive control. The judgment of Roberts J shows what can be done, creatively and holistically, in cases where predatory marriage is a concern.

The law in respect of predatory marriage is in its infancy, the decision of Roberts J in *Re BU* will be a cornerstone of the approach taken by the courts as this area develops.

The *Hinduja* litigation (the history of which is explained by the Court of Appeal in [2022] EWCA Civ 1492) dispels any myth that the health and welfare of high net worth individuals does not come before the Court of Protection.

Equally, the number of high net worth individuals whose care and support arrangements amount to a deprivation of liberty in their own homes is simply unknown. The suspicion of Court of Protection practitioners is that the numbers are significant. With regard to those individuals who are deprived of their liberty in care homes, many high net worth individuals will not have the benefit of an authorisation under schedule A1 of the Mental Capacity Act 2005. Sometimes this is an issue of the capacity of local statutory services, on other occasions it is a misunderstanding as to the legal status of self-funding residents.

The potential risk to individuals living in the community, with issues as to their mental capacity, are more broadly known and discussed following the enactment of the Mental Capacity Act 2005. The development of the case law in respect of individuals who are deprived of their liberty outside of care homes and hospitals has further advanced that discussion. Less discussed is the phenomenon of what is sometimes called, "mate crime", where individuals are targeted for exploitation in the community due to their disability. In some cases, "mate crime" has had tragic consequences and the issue of mental capacity has loomed large.[2]

It is not only the Court of Protection that will have to deal with these societal issues but attorneys and deputies too. The sad reality, demonstrated by the decision of Arbuthnot J in her recent decision in *CA*[3], is that some attorneys pose a risk to the person who they are supposed to be assisting.

The Senior Judge of the Court of Protection, Her Honour Judge Hilder has carefully delivered a number of judgments to ensure that deputies for property and affairs do not go beyond the decision-making authority given to them by the Court.

The question, which rightly will be asked, is why these issues are particular to health and welfare cases involving high net worth individuals. The simple answer is that they are not unique to such cases but some issues appear with greater frequency.

High net worth individuals are more likely to be cared for in their own home; often their care and support arrangements do not involve statutory services and it follows that they are less likely to have been scrutinised by the Court of Protection, even when those care and support arrangements amount to a deprivation of liberty. Even though a state body may not be funding those care and support arrangements, they may still be imputable to the state and require authorisation to accord with Article 5 of the European Convention on Human Rights.

---

2 See for example the safeguarding adults review in Camden in 2023 in respect of "Matthew" : https://nationalnetwork.org.uk/2023/Camden%20SAR%20Matthew%20Final%20Report%20April%202023.pdf

3 [2024] EWCOP 64 (T3)

Despite having significant financial resources, an individual may be at more risk of an infringement of their rights, or being exploited, simply because of the lack of oversight from public bodies. Some issues have rarely been considered by the Court of Protection, for example, privately funded medical treatment. At times, the statutory roles of local authorities and NHS bodies is unclear, or is misunderstood, especially when they are not actively involved in a person's life.

Ultimately, the failure of statutory bodies, or the conduct of individuals before and during health and welfare proceedings may result in adverse consequences including the award of costs against them. This book concludes with an exploration of the circumstances in which the court may disapply the usual rule in health and welfare proceedings that each party pays their own costs.

Throughout this book, some misconceptions are highlighted. The hope in writing this book is that by introducing people to the issues that systems and practices will adapt.

CHAPTER TWO

THE DECISION-MAKING AUTHORITY OF A PROPERTY AND AFFAIRS DEPUTY

Introduction

This book does not address the decision-making authority of a deputy for health and welfare matters. Through practice, and following the decision in *Re Lawson, Mottram and Hopton (appointment of personal welfare deputies)*[4], they remain relatively rare.

More common are property and affairs deputies who are managing the estates of high net worth individuals. The identities of the property and affairs deputy will vary, some are professionals, others are professionals who take the work through a panel operated by the Office of the Public Guardian and some will be family members or friends of the person who lacks the mental capacity to make decisions as to their property and affairs.

The scope of a deputy's decision-making authority remains something which is misunderstood. Professional deputies, especially those managing large personal injury awards, are increasingly being brought into health and welfare cases before the Court of Protection. This chapter looks at the scope of a property and affairs deputy's decision-making ability.

---

4 [2019] EWCOP 22

The basic concept of a deputy

Whilst lasting powers of attorney are often featured in the media, deputies get less attention. Sometimes, social and healthcare professionals working with an individual will use the terms "attorney" and "deputy" interchangeably, this is incorrect.

The most recent media focus on deputyships, and how they operate in England and Wales. actually arose from a case involving a high net worth individual overseas. In 2021, the #FreeBritney campaign came to an end as the Superior Court of California brought to an end the conservatorship in relation to pop star, Britney Spears. Whilst the Californian concept of conservatorship is different to deputyship in England and Wales, a worldwide discussion was started.

The elementary equation in respect of deputyship is as follows:

(1) A person lacks the mental capacity to make a decision, or a number of decisions;

(2) The court determines that it is in the person's best interests to appoint a deputy to make the decision(s);

(3) The court makes an order appointing a deputy and gives them such powers or duties as necessary;

(4) The deputy then makes the decision(s) in P's best interests.

The important core aspects are therefore:

(1) What decisions has the person been assessed as not being able to make in accordance with sections 2 and 3 of the Mental Capacity Act 2005?

(2) Which decisions (if any) has the court made on the person's behalf and which are to be made by the deputy in accordance with section 16(2) of the Mental Capacity Act 2005?

(3) What additional powers or duties are included within the court's order as per section 16(5) of the Mental Capacity Act 2005?

Section 18 of the Mental Capacity Act 2005 gives specific examples of the types of property and affairs decisions which may be made under section 16 (and as a corollary by a property and affairs deputy).

Section 19 of the Mental Capacity Act 2005 specifies who may become a deputy and provides more detail as to their appointment. Section 20 of the Mental Capacity Act 2005 sets out the restrictions in respect of the scope of a deputy's decision-making authority.

Paragraph 8.54 of the Mental Capacity Act 2005 Code of Practice reminds deputies that they must only make decisions which the court has empowered them to make.

Despite the foregoing, the court has had cause to examine the issue in detail.

ACC & Ors and cases which have followed

In 2020, the Senior Judge of the Court of Protection, Her Honour Judge Hilder, delivered her decision in *ACC & Ors (property and affairs deputy; recovering assets costs for legal proceedings)*[5]. That was a decision in respect of three joined cases, the primary issue being whether, and in what circumstances, a property and affairs deputy can recover from

---

5 [2020] EWCOP 9 (27 February 2020)

the protected person's assets costs which have been, or are likely to be, incurred in legal proceedings.

The court outlined that the standard deputyship order, which the court generally will make, gives a 'general' authority to manage P's property and affairs. The court was clear that this authority only encompasses those tasks which are required to administer P's estate efficiently.

With regard to obtaining legal advice, the court held that the authority conferred by 'general' authority is limited. That limitation is to non-contentious legal tasks, including obtaining legal advice, as are ancillary to giving effect to the general authority.

However, it is apparent from both the judgment and wider practice, that it was known that property and affairs deputies had proceeded on the basis that their general authority entitled them to litigate on P's behalf. The court held that this was not so; if a property and affairs deputy seeks to embark on litigation, they must first seek specific authority from the Court of Protection. This is subject to exceptions.

A property and affairs deputy *can* bring Court of Protection proceedings in respect of a property and affairs issue without prior authority of the court.[6]

And, a property and affairs deputy could and should bring Court of Protection proceedings in respect of health and welfare matters without prior authority of the court, if[7]:

> *having been properly alerted by the property and affairs deputy, the appropriate body or institution drags its heels in referring a*

6 Paragraph 52.4 of *ACC*

7 Paragraph 52.10 of *ACC*

> *non-property-and-affairs issue to court, the deputy may – without specific authority to do so – appropriately make an application to draw this to the attention of the court and seek further directions. Moreover, the deputy should do so.*

However, the court was helpfully direct as to the scope of a property and affairs deputy's role[8]:

> *a property and affairs deputyship does not confer any authority in respect of welfare. If a welfare issue arises, there may be a body or institution more appropriately placed than the property and affairs deputy to make that application, at less cost to P.*

The distinction between property and affairs decisions and those which relate to health and welfare is not always clear. This is something to which Her Honour Judge Hilder referred[9] in her judgment.

The decision in *ACC* was something to which the court returned in *PSG Trust Corporation Ltd v CK & Anor.*[10] In that case, Mr Justice Hayden had to determine the issue of whether to inform P of the value of their civil litigation settlement. During the course of his judgment, Hayden J returned to the divide between a property and affairs decision and health and welfare. He stated, speaking of *ACC*[11]:

> *What is in issue is communication of the exact sum of a damages award. That strikes me as a property and affairs matter. The fact that welfare considerations flow from it does not change the*

---

8 Paragraph 52.5 of *ACC*

9 Paragraph 52.6 of *ACC*

10 [2024] EWCOP 14

11 Paragraph 31 of *TSG*

> *nature of the matter. Many financial issues have welfare implications, taking out mortgages, finance agreements, sustaining an extensive overdraft. This view seems to me to be entirely consistent with Judge Hilder's observations, indeed, she uses the term "in the realm of property and affairs" which implicitly recognises that decisions in that sphere will sometimes have welfare implications. I do not believe, therefore, that it is necessary to extend a deputy's authority in every case. Neither, however, do I wish to be prescriptive. Precisely because the Court of Protection is such a highly fact-specific jurisdiction, it is perfectly conceivable that what might appear on the surface to be a Property and Affairs issue, is on a proper construction, nothing of the kind and truly a welfare issue. In these cases, an application can be made and a deputy's authority extended where appropriate.*

Most recently, the Senior Judge returned to the authority of a property and affairs deputy in *Lumb v NHS Humber and North Yorkshire ICB & Anor*[12]. In that case the focus was upon what involvement a property and affairs deputy can/should have in the management of a Personal Health Budget under the National Health Service (Direct Payments) Regulations 2013.

Ultimately, HHJ Hilder Senior Judge Hilder answered the question of whether the management of direct payments comes within the standard authorisations of a deputyship appointment; or, if it does not, whether such authorisation might be specifically granted. HHJ Hilder concluded that 'representative' for the purposes of Personal Health Budget direct payments has to[13]:

---

12 [2024] EWCOP 57 (T2)

13 Paragraph 69 of *Lumb*

> *be able to 'plan' care arrangements – as in 'devise' them, not simply make administrative arrangements to pay for them. Such 'planning' of care arrangements is* ***not*** *within the standard authorisations of a property and affairs deputy*

For completeness, HHJ Hilder concluded[14] that a case manager *could* be appointed as a 'representative' in this regard.

Specific practice points in respect of high net worth individuals

Case managers

The role of case manager does not appear in the Mental Capacity Act 2005. Case managers often feature in cases where a person has been awarded damages as part of a personal injury or clinical negligence claim. Case managers will sometimes feature in the privately funded care and support arrangements of older individuals, or in complex care packages commissioned by statutory bodies.

The role of the case manager and how they operate in litigation is a matter for another book. However, in brief, the case manager will work with the lawyers bringing a damages claim (if there is one) and other health and social care professionals. The role of a case manager is facilitative, they will help co-ordinate the multi-disciplinary team to ensure the needs of the client, and their family, are being met.

The case manager's role is not as a surrogate social worker in respect of a privately funded package of care. The case manager does not have any decision-making authority beyond the person who is instructing them. A case manager who is instructed by a property and affairs

14 Paragraph 107(e) of *Lumb.*

deputy does not have health and welfare decision-making authority that the deputy does not possess.

Equally, case managers cannot be expected to assume the role of statutory services, especially in respect of safeguarding adults. However, the appointment of a case manager is sometimes used as a means of avoiding, or reducing, conflict in respect of privately funded care packages for high net worth individuals. The idea being that the case manager will provide an independent view as to the arrangements and act as a conduit. It follows that sometimes a case manager will provide witness evidence in health and welfare proceedings before the Court of Protection.

Deputies being made parties in health and welfare proceedings

Property and affairs deputies are not automatically made parties in health and welfare proceedings. However, there is increasingly a trend for them to be joined to those proceedings, especially in cases involving high net worth individuals.

High net worth individuals will often fall outside of the financial eligibility criteria for state funded care. In those cases, the property and affairs deputy will often be the individual who is able to identify alternative options for where a person lives, or what care they receive. This is squarely in the remit of a deputy for property and affairs, applying the decision in *ACC*. However, it does not follow that the deputy for property and affairs needs to be a party to proceedings. Indeed, there are costs implications for P which have to be justified. The deputy can be provided with documents, as can the Public Guardian using the various provision in Part 5 of the Court of Protection Rules 2017. Part 9 of the Court of Protection Rules 2017 deals with party status, there is no automatic requirement for a deputy for property and affairs to become a party in health and welfare proceedings even if they are responsible for commissioning alternative options for P's residence and care.

Property and affairs deputies are called upon to provide evidence in health and welfare cases which have safeguarding elements.

Consultation

Whilst a property and affairs deputy may not be the decision maker in respect of a particular decision which P is unable to make with regard to their health and welfare, the deputy may still be someone to be consulted.

Often professional deputies may have had long term involvement with P and their family, especially in cases where there is significant family wealth, or the deputy has been involved over the lifetime of a claim. The fact that the deputy is appointed for property and affairs does not prevent their consultation in respect of health and welfare matters.

In respect of attorneys, the Mental Capacity Act 2005 Code of Practice suggests[15] that it is, 'good practice' to consult an attorney even if it's not an area in which decision making has been granted to them. The same must be true for deputies, it is arguably good practice to consult a property and affairs deputy about a health and welfare decision. Section 4(7)(d) of the Mental Capacity Act 2005 requires such consultation if it is practicable and appropriate.

15 Paragraph 7.57

Deprivation of liberty

Many high net worth individuals have extensive care and support packages in their own home, or other community settings which amount to a deprivation of their liberty. Many of these care and support packages go without the scrutiny of public bodies and some are not authorised by the Court of Protection. This is addressed in Chapter Six.

Where a property and affairs deputy is commissioning care arrangements for a person which satisfy the 'acid test,' to which the person cannot consent, then often it will be necessary to secure authorisation for the deprivation of liberty which arises. In such a case, the deputy will alert the local authority with safeguarding responsibilities for the person to make enquiries and, ultimately, an application to the Court of Protection if necessary: *SSJ v Staffordshire County Council*[16].

Summary

(1) A property and affairs deputy does not have the authority to make decisions as to health and welfare matters;

(2) It is good practice to consult with a property and affairs deputy about a health and welfare matter if it is reasonable and practicable to do so;

(3) Property and affairs deputies may bring litigation on behalf of P subject to the decision in *ACC*. Property and affairs deputies do not have the general power to litigate on behalf of P;

16 [2016] EWCA Civ 1317

(4) Case managers do not have powers to make decisions beyond those of the person instructing them.

CHAPTER THREE

LASTING POWERS OF ATTORNEY FOR HEALTH AND WELFARE

Introduction

There are two kinds of lasting power of attorney, one for health and welfare, another for property and affairs. The latter is outside of the remit of this book, however, some helpful insight might be drawn from the contents of Chapter Two in respect of deputies for property and affairs.

The number of lasting powers of attorney ('LPAs') have increased in recent years, some are prepared by legal professionals, others are not. As the number of LPAs increases, as will the number of Court of Protection cases which consider their validity and the decisions made by attorneys.

High net worth individuals will often consider future decision making in respect of their health and welfare alongside broader estate planning.

The basic concept of an attorney

A lasting power of attorney (LPA) is a document which allows an individual with mental capacity (the 'donor') to appoint one or more people ('attorneys')[17] to make decisions on their behalf. In respect of

[17] In the Mental Capacity Act 2005 they are referred to as donees.

health and welfare, this is a form of forward planning. The donor decides on a decision maker, in future, where they lack capacity to make a decision for themselves.

Before a person is able to use a LPA it has to be registered with the Office of the Public Guardian ('OPG'). The OPG is responsible for overseeing the registration and operation of LPAs.

The gov.uk website[18] gives four examples of types of decision which a health and welfare attorney might make:

- *your daily routine, for example washing, dressing, eating*
- *medical care*
- *moving into a care home*
- *life-sustaining treatment*

The Mental Capacity Act Code of Practice provides a broader set of examples:

> *Personal welfare LPAs might include decisions about:*
>
> - *where the donor should live and who they should live with*
> - *the donor's day-to-day care, including diet and dress*
> - *who the donor may have contact with*

[18] https://www.gov.uk/power-of-attorney

- *consenting to or refusing medical examination and treatment on the donor's behalf*
- *arrangements needed for the donor to be given medical, dental or optical treatment*
- *assessments for and provision of community care services*
- *whether the donor should take part in social activities, leisure activities, education or training*
- *the donor's personal correspondence and papers*
- *rights of access to personal information about the donor, or*
- *complaints about the donor's care or treatment.*

Section 11 of the Mental Capacity Act 2005 is clear that a health and welfare decision cannot be made on behalf of P, using the lasting power of attorney, unless there is reason to believe that the individual lacks the mental capacity to make the decision for themselves.

Specific practice points in respect of high net worth individuals

Creation of the LPA

As stated above, it is not unusual for a high net worth individual to consider their future health and welfare as part of their wider estate planning. However, there remain a number of cases where individuals purportedly execute lasting powers of attorney in hospitals, or registered care settings, especially following an acute medical event. There is nothing within the Mental Capacity Act 2005, Mental Capacity Act Code of Practice or the caselaw which prevents an instrument being executed in such a setting, but it does sometimes raise questions as to the validity of the document.

For the instrument to be valid, the individual granting the lasting power of attorney must have the capacity to execute the document as per section 11(2)(c) of the Mental Capacity Act 2005. The execution of instruments when a person is in hospital, or is in a care setting may become contentious later.

The lasting power of attorney has an inbuilt safety mechanism, provided for in paragraph 2(1)(e) of schedule 1 of the Mental Capacity Act 2005. For a lasting power of attorney to be valid an individual known as a certificate provider signs the LPA after the donor and the donor's witness. The certificate provider's role is to certify that the donor: (i) understands the scope of the authority they are granting and the purpose of the LPA; (ii) they are not being subject to fraud or undue pressure to create a LPA and (iii) there is nothing else which would prevent a lasting power of attorney from being created by the instrument.

There are limits as to who can act as a certificate provider to avoid any conflict of interest. For example, the person to whom powers are being granted cannot act as the certificate provider.

The role of a certificate provider is not insignificant. It is not as simple as witnessing the signature on the instrument, or asking the donor if they are content. Lieven J recently explored the issue in *TA v The Public Guardian*[19]:

> *29. Paragraph 2(1)(e) requires the provision of a certificate, but it also requires that certificate to have particular content. The content is that the certificate provider has an opinion as to three*

[19] [2023] EWCOP 63

> *specific matters. Therefore, on a pure black letter law approach, a valid certificate must be based on an opinion as to those three matters. If the evidence showed that the certificate provider did not have such an opinion because, for example, they had not spoken to the donor, then there would not be a valid opinion.*
>
> *30. It therefore follows from the words themselves that the Court is entitled to check that the requisite opinion has actually been formed…*

The attorney

A recurring theme in cases involving lasting powers of attorney granted by high net worth individuals is *who* is selected to be the attorney. Two common contentious appointments are: (i) where one child (or family member) is appointed and others are not; (ii) when an individual outside of the family is selected, perhaps a recent partner, a neighbour or an employee.

There is no requirement that a person selects:

(i) a family member to act as an attorney;

(ii) a person who is ordinarily resident in the United Kingdom;

(iii) a particular family member, there is no requirement to select the eldest child, or all the children for example;

(iv) the same person to act as a property affairs attorney and a health and welfare attorney.

A bankrupt person may be appointed as an attorney for health and welfare but *not* as an attorney for property and financial affairs as per section 10(3) of the Mental Capacity Act 2005. The other requirement is that the attorney has reached the age of 18.

Health and welfare attorneys who live in different jurisdictions, or multiple jurisdictions is not uncommon in cases involving high net worth individuals. Whilst it may pose logistical challenges, it is not impermissible.[20] A common problem is the failure to consult with the health and welfare attorney or to recognise their decision-making authority, this is especially so when they are outside of the jurisdiction.

The failure to consult with an attorney

There is a lack of consistent training for health and social care professionals in respect of the decision-making authority of attorneys and the need to consult with them. This is not an issue which is unique to cases involving high net worth individuals. It can though be a particular issue where a public body becomes involved (perhaps through safeguarding) with private care packages that are being directed by a health and welfare attorney.

A health and welfare attorney's decision-making authority is not limitless. It is limited by section 11 of the Mental Capacity Act 2005 and what the instrument itself actually provides for. It is important that anyone exercising decision-making authority under a lasting power of attorney is aware of what decision-making authority the instrument provides. Equally, any person purportedly making a best interests decision under section 4 of the Mental Capacity Act 2005 should assure themselves that they are entitled to make the decision and it is not one which is provided for by the instrument.

20 See the judgment of the previous Senior Judge in *DGP Law v DGHP & Ors* [2015] EWCOP 58

Even if a health and welfare attorney is not entitled to make a particular decision that P cannot make for themselves, they still ought to be consulted by the decision maker where it is appropriate and practicable to do so as per section 4(7)(c) of the Mental Capacity Act 2005.

The decisions made by health and welfare attorneys

A health and welfare attorney is only able to make a decision that P themselves lacks the capacity to make. Health and social care professionals should not defer to attorneys in circumstances where the individual is able to make decisions for themselves. If an attorney for health and welfare is making a decision using the power given to them by an instrument, they should satisfy themselves (and be prepared to satisfy others and the court) that P lacks the mental capacity to make that particular decision.

An attorney when making a decision using the authority given to them by the lasting power of attorney should apply the factors in the best interests checklist in section 4 of the Mental Capacity Act 2005. The attorney ought to consult, just as they ought to be consulted.

Should an attorney act in a way that is not in P's best interests, or proposes to act in a way that is not in P's best interests, then the court may revoke the lasting power of attorney using the power in section 22(4)(b) of the Mental Capacity Act 2005. That power depends on P themselves lacking the mental capacity to revoke the instrument.

Applications to revoke a lasting power of attorney

An application to revoke a lasting powering of attorney due to the behaviour of the attorney does not have to be brought by the Public Guardian. Any person may bring the application, the Court of

Protection will consider whether to grant the applicant the permission to bring proceedings in accordance with section 50(3) of the Mental Capacity Act 2005. A common example is when local authorities bring applications to revoke lasting powers of attorney due to their safeguarding duties, even if an individual is receiving only privately funded or informal care.

In the Matter Of CA (Fact Finding – Capacity – Inherent Jurisdiction – Injunctive Relief[21], Arbuthnot J used the inherent jurisdiction of the High Court to make injunctions to prevent the use of a lasting power of attorney where P *had* the mental capacity to revoke the instrument but was subject to coercion and did not do so.

Summary

(1) An attorney may make a decision on behalf of a person who lacks capacity to make the decision for themselves;

(2) The attorney does not have to live in the United Kingdom;

(3) Where appropriate and practicable, the attorney should consult with others before making a decision on P's behalf. Equally, the attorney should be consulted where appropriate and practicable even if they are not the decision maker;

(4) The Court of Protection may make orders to revoke a lasting power of attorney, anybody may make an application in this regard, it is not limited to the Public Guardian. Often it will be the local authority who makes this application pursuant to their safeguarding duties.

21 [2024] EWCOP 64 (T3)

CHAPTER FOUR

PRIVATELY FUNDED CARE AND SUPPORT ARRANGEMENTS

Introduction

The cost of care and who funds it is a politically contentious topic. Legally, the assessment as to whether an individual is eligible for state funded care may be complex. In this chapter, common issues in respect of privately funded care and support arrangements are explored. The reality being that wealthier individuals are much more likely to privately fund their own care and support arrangements.

The basic concept of care and support arrangements

In the simplest sense, care and support arrangements are those which relate to helping a person live their life. Those arrangements can relate to what might be considered mundane, for example helping someone to wash or dress. Or, they can relate to something more alarming, for example preventing a person from being subject to financial or sexual exploitation.

Care and support is delivered in a variety of different ways in diverse settings. The terminology in this area may be unfamiliar:

Care plan: A document which outlines the care and support which will be provided to a person.

CHC: NHS Continuing Healthcare is a package of care for adults aged 18 or over which is arranged and funded solely by the NHS.

FNC: NHS-funded nursing care is when the NHS pays for the nursing care component of nursing home fees.

Residential care home: Registered care settings which provide accommodation and personal care.

Nursing home: Registered care setting which provides accommodation and personal care, there will be nursing staff available on site.

Discharge to assess: Following a period of time in hospital, a person is discharged to a care setting so that their care needs may be assessed.

Domiciliary care: range of services put in place to support an individual in their own home.

Specific practice points in respect of high net worth individuals

Costs of care

The costs of a care package are often at the centre of disputes. Many high net worth individuals will not be entitled to state funded care. As a result, their care will be funded by their estate, or, sometimes by the wider family.

There is no obligation on the person arranging and commissioning the care to minimise the cost with a view to protecting the potential inheritance to be received by others. Rather, the costs of different care packages will be factors to be considered when determining which care package is in an individual's best interests.

Disputes as to the costs of a care package can be avoided if there is a rigorous approach taken to identifying and commissioning a private care package. Unfortunately, the exigencies of life are such that rarely people take that approach.

A common situation eventuates with older people. As a high net worth person gets older, they (or their family) may start to recognise that they require increased help with the activities of daily living so that they are able to remain living in their own home. At first that might be adaptations to properties, or, the use of technological solutions. As time goes on, carers may come into the home, or respite provision at a care home arranged.

Often care packages for high net worth individuals grow organically, without the intervention or oversight of the state. When disputes arise as to why particular decisions were made as to care provision, there is often very little by way of documentation to support the decision making. In those circumstances, there are often arguments that too much is being spent on care provision, or, sometimes not enough.

Where the disputes reach the Court of Protection, it is usual for the court to order: (i) an assessment of the individual's care and support needs; (ii) the identification of the available options which may be able to meet those needs; (iii) an analysis of which of those options is in the individual's best interests. This work can be done ahead of proceedings being issued in the Court of Protection and before any dispute arises. Unfortunately, it is rare that such preparatory steps are taken.

Live in care

It is very rare for a state funded package of care to involve care provision in a person's home for twenty four hours a day. It is not uncommon in cases involving high net worth individuals.

Live in care arrangements can sometimes be features in health and welfare cases before the Court of Protection. Certain issues feature frequently in respect of those arrangements:

(i) The use of CCTV within the home. It is not uncommon for cameras to be set up in a person's home; why they are being set up and who is able to access them is sometimes contentious.

(ii) Privacy. Live in carers are sharing the same space as the person they care for. Family members of the person being cared for often have expectations that they will be able to spend time in the company of their loved one without the carer being present.

(iii) Respite. Live in carers are entitled to periods of holiday or sick leave like any other carer. The nature of respite provision for those periods of time can cause disputes, especially where it is proposed that a family member takes over the care, or, if the individual will spend a period of time in a care home.

(iv) Allegations against the carer. Frequently, in these circumstances, the local authority will first come to be involved in a person's care and support arrangements when allegations are made against a carer. Such allegations, and the safeguarding enquiry that follows, may cause the live in care package to be destabilised or for it to be changed in some way.

The Care Quality Commission (CQC) which regulates all health and adult social care services in England expects that care will be provided in a safe way which respects the rights of the person receiving the care. Anybody commissioning care from a live in carer will be expected to ensure that there are such policies and procedures in place as are necessary to safely deliver the care required.

The fact that a person is living within their own home, with a package of care commissioned from their own funds is not an indicator that a person is not being deprived of their liberty. This is addressed in the chapter on deprivation of liberty.

Home as an available option

In cases where an individual's care and support arrangements amount to a deprivation of liberty, that has to be authorised by the court, or by schedule A1 of the Mental Capacity Act 2005. Where a person is subject to a deprivation of liberty under schedule A1 of the Mental Capacity Act 2005, they have the right to access the court to challenge their care and support arrangements under section 21A of the Mental Capacity Act 2005.

When such challenges are brought, the court will consider what the available options are to meet the individual's care needs. There is sometimes a reluctance to consider whether a person may leave a hospital or a care home to return home. Often arguments centre around whether a person's needs are able to be met in their own home. It is vital that there is a consideration of whether a person's estate may be used for their benefit to fund care and make adaptations so that can be made an available option.

Summary

(1) A high net worth individual is much more likely to fund their own care and support arrangements.

(2) That care and support may be delivered in a variety of ways, this might include delivery of care in their own home. A person's care and support arrangements in their own home may still amount to a deprivation of liberty.

(3) The cost of care packages is often a source of tension and dispute. Those disagreements may be avoided if care is taken to properly identify a person's needs and why they are being met in a particular way.

(4) Live in care is not a common feature of state funded care. However, it is more common when high net worth individuals are funding their own care, practical issues arise with this model of care which may result in disputes before the Court of Protection.

(5) A return home should not be discounted as an available option when a person is being discharged from hospital or objecting to being in a care home. Thought should be given to whether the person's estate can be used to make adaptations or deliver care in their home.

CHAPTER FIVE

PRIVATELY FUNDED MEDICAL TREATMENT, INCLUDING COSMETIC PROCEDURES

Introduction

Publicly available data shows that the vast majority of planned health care in England is delivered by the NHS. In 2021/22, the most recent full year for which data is available, 13% of medical care was funded privately.

The British Medical Association produces specific guidance for doctors who are setting up in private practice[22], it highlights the contractual relationship between a doctor and patient. It also stresses that the cost of treatment is something to which they must consent.

This chapter explores practice points around privately funded medical care including what happens when there is a dispute as to a patient's mental capacity to consent to treatment, or, if treatment is in their best interests.

The basic concept of consent to medical treatment, including cosmetic procedures

Many of the published judgments from the Court of Protection relate to what is described as, "serious medical treatment." Whether it is

[22] https://www.bma.org.uk/advice-and-support/private-practice/setting-up-in-private-practice/setting-up-in-private-practice-overview

serious or not, the basic concept of consent applies to all medical treatment.

The law assumes that an adult has the mental capacity to consent to medical treatment unless it is shown that they do not: section 1(2) of the Mental Capacity Act 2005.

The expectation on healthcare professionals is that they obtain consent from patients who have the capacity to give it any time they wish to initiate an examination, treatment, or any other intervention. Consent may be expressed or implied, it will only be valid if the patient has the mental capacity to provide that consent.

In the context of privately funded medical treatment, this will very likely be planned examinations or treatment. Patients need to understand that they can refuse the proposed treatment or examination, as do they need to understand the risks and benefits of what is proposed.

To assess a person's mental capacity to consent to a particular treatment, it is necessary to identify the relevant information for the purposes of section 3 of the Mental Capacity Act 2005. For a person to have capacity to consent they need to understand, retain, use or weigh the relevant information. The relevant information will include the nature, purpose and effects of the proposed treatment, the last of these entailing information as to the benefits and risks of deciding to have or not to have the operation, or of not making a decision at all.

The assessment will be specific to the particular patient and the particular proposed treatment. The patient, *"is not required to understand every last piece of information about her situation and her options: even her doctors would not make that claim. It must also be remembered that common strategies for dealing with unpalatable dilemmas – for example indecision, avoidance or vacillation – are not to be confused with incapacity. We should not ask more of people whose capacity is questioned than of those whose capacity is undoubted."*[23]

Arguably, any privately funded medical care will need to include a person understanding the cost of the procedure (if there is any) and whether it can be delivered alternatively by the NHS.

Consent in respect of cosmetic procedures includes the same concepts as outlined above. In some cases, the relevant information may need to include that particular procedures require repetition. For some patients there may be particular risks or benefits relating to their mental health following a cosmetic procedure, again, that may need to be included in the relevant information.

The basic concept of best interests decision making in respect of medical treatment, including cosmetic procedures

It is important to emphasise from the outset, that the patient, and the Court of Protection, cannot force healthcare professionals to provide treatment or investigations which they are not willing to provide. Rather, the best interests decision-making process is about deciding between available options.

The concept of best interests is not defined within the Mental Capacity Act 2005, rather there is a checklist of factors to be considered in section 4. Again, these factors will be tailored to the particular patient and the treatment which is being contemplated.

A best interests analysis is not designed to determine what the patient would have determined themselves if they had capacity. However, the

23 Paragraph 26 of the judgment of Peter Jackson J (as he then was) in *Heart of England NHS Foundation Trust v JB* [2014] EWCOP 342

person making the best interests decision is required to consider the patient's expressed wishes and feelings both at the time the decision is being made and in the past. Those wishes and feelings are very important, the Court of Appeal put it this way[24]:

> *"part of the underlying ethos of the Mental Capacity Act 2005 is that those making decisions for people who may be lacking capacity must respect and maximise that person's individuality and autonomy to the greatest possible extent. In order to achieve this aim, a person's wishes and feelings not only require consideration, but can be determinative, even if they lack capacity."*

The NHS produce a helpful advice document in respect of cosmetic procedures which may be a helpful means for guiding discussions with a patient as to their wishes and feelings.[25]

Specific practice points in respect of high net worth individuals

Transferring between NHS and private providers

One of the common requests in health and welfare proceedings is for people to transfer their treatment from the NHS to private providers or *vice versa*. There is nothing in the NHS Constitution for England or the NHS Wales Core Principles which prevents such a transfer of treatment, indeed both documents would require the NHS body to be facilitative of a transfer. If a patient has had private treatment abroad, they should be permitted to access follow up treatment in the

---

[24] Paragraph 71 of the judgment of King LJ in *AB (Termination of Pregnancy)* [2019] EWCA Civ 1215

[25] https://www.nhs.uk/conditions/cosmetic-procedures/advice/cosmetic-procedure-right-for-me/

United Kingdom, be it through their general practitioner or referral to a specialist NHS service if required.

However, a simple demand to transfer treatment into or out of the NHS does not mean that it will be facilitated. The first question is whether the treatment or investigation is available at an alternative provider, if the proposed transfer is to a private provider then it will only be an available option if there is a means to fund it. If there is an available alternative option, a question will then follow as to whether the patient has the mental capacity to make the decision to transfer their care. This, as with any best interests analysis, will need to take into account factors specific to the proposed treatment. It is not as a simple as stating that private healthcare is better than that provided by the NHS. This may not be true.

There may, for example, be issues as to escalating care if a patient has an adverse reaction to anaesthesia, or whether the proposed alternative provider has staff who are able to deal with the patient's particular needs.

Cosmetic procedures

Decisions about cosmetic procedures are not regularly decided upon by the Court of Protection; unlike other aspects of medical treatment there is no canon of caselaw to which healthcare professionals and those advising them can refer.

What is clear is that the cosmetic result of a particular treatment is something which the court may consider in a best interests analysis, see for example the decision of Hayden J in *Sherwood Forest Hospitals NHS Foundation Trust & Anor v H.*[26]

Deputies for property and affairs may be faced with requests to fund cosmetic procedures from a patient's estate. Such a decision is likely to involve questions as to both the patient's property and affairs and their health and welfare, the deputy will need to carefully consider their decision-making authority in this regard. A property and affairs deputy could not consent to the procedure on the patient's behalf, see Chapters Two and Three in respect of the position of deputies and attorneys.

Primarily the role of a deputy (or attorney) for property and affairs would be to identify whether the individual could afford the treatment from their estate so that it could become an available option. A best interests decision making process will need to be undertaken if the patient is unable to consent to the proposed treatment.

Just because somebody lacks the mental capacity to make a decision as to cosmetic treatment, it does not follow that the matter will have to be referred to the Court of Protection for a decision. Those involved in the decision will need to have regard to the Serious Medical Treatment Guidance[27] and determine if an application is necessary.

---

[26] [2020] EWCOP 5

[27] [2020] EWCOP 2

Summary

(1) The law assumes that an adult has the mental capacity to consent to medical treatment unless it is proved otherwise.

(2) The relevant information in respect of a proposed treatment or investigation will need to be tailored to the particular patient and their circumstances when conducting a mental capacity assessment.

(3) A best interests analysis of whether a proposed treatment or investigation is in a patient's best interests will give significant weight to the patient's wishes and feelings.

(4) Transfer of treatment between private and NHS providers is possible if funding is available and should be facilitated if it is in the patient's best interests.

(5) Deputies and attorneys will have to carefully consider whether they are the decision maker in respect of any proposed cosmetic procedure, the starting point is to determine whether the patient can make the decision for themselves.

CHAPTER SIX

DEPRIVATION OF LIBERTY

Introduction

Care and support arrangements which amount to a deprivation of a person's liberty are a common feature of health and welfare cases before the Court of Protection. The majority of cases relate to individuals who are receiving care in registered care settings, some relate to individuals who are living in the community and receiving care and support.

There were an estimated 332,455 applications for DOLS received during 2023-24. This is an increase of 11% similar to the previous year.[28] These applications only relate to individuals in care homes and hospitals, outside of that there will be a further cohort of persons who have been subject to court applications to authorise the deprivation of liberty arising from their care and support arrangements in the community.

The demographics recorded in respect of these processes do not differentiate between those who are privately funding their arrangements and those whose care and support arrangements are being funded by the state. The suspicion, amongst Court of Protection practitioners at least, is that there remain significant numbers of

[28] https://digital.nhs.uk/data-and-information/publications/statistical/mental-capacity-act-2005-deprivation-of-liberty-safeguards-assessments/2023-24

individuals who are deprived of their liberty without any form of authorisation.

The basic concept of a deprivation of liberty

Other books focus on the concept of a deprivation of liberty and deprivation of liberty safeguards ("DOLS") in detail, this is a simple introduction to those who are unfamiliar with the concept. Here, the focus is upon when a deprivation of liberty may arise from the care, support or treatment arrangements of an adult in England and Wales.

A person will be deprived of their liberty for the purposes of Article 5(1) of the European Convention on Human Rights when: (1) they are confined to (subject to continuous supervision and control and not free to leave) a particular place for a non-negligible period of time; (2) they do not or cannot consent to that confinement; and (3) that confinement is imputable to the state.

A judgment of the Supreme Court in 2014[29] provided an "acid test" for what constitutes a "deprivation of liberty".

The acid test states that an individual is deprived of their liberty for the purposes of Article 5 of the European Convention on Human Rights if they:

- lack the capacity to consent to their care / treatment arrangements
- are under continuous supervision and control

---

[29] *P (by his litigation friend the Official Solicitor) v Cheshire West and Chester Council & Anor* [2014] UKSC 19 – Court of Protection practitioners and social workers will often refer to this as, "Cheshire West".

- are not free to leave

All three elements must be present for the acid test to be met.

In the context of this book, a person cannot consent to that confinement if they lack the mental capacity to do so. For those people who are in a registered care setting, or hospital, the statutory test is whether the person has capacity, *"in relation to the question whether or not he should be accommodated in the relevant hospital or care home for the purpose of being given the relevant care or treatment."*[30]

The approach taken by Baker J (as he then was) in *A Primary Care Trust v LDV & Ors* [2013] EWHC 272 (Fam) is generally applied when assessing a person's capacity in this regard, that being that a person has to be able to understand, use or weigh, and retain the core elements of the confinement to which the person is subject.

The imputability of the confinement to the state is a particularly important issue in cases involving high net worth individuals and is addressed in more detail below.

How a deprivation of liberty is authorised

For adults in England and Wales who lack the mental capacity to make decisions as to their care and support arrangements, there are two primary mechanisms[31] by which the deprivation of liberty which arises from those arrangements may be authorised.

---

30 Paragraph 15 of Schedule A1 of the Mental Capacity Act 2005

31 The inherent jurisdiction of the High Court is sometimes used to authorise deprivations of liberty, see for example the decision of Theis J in *Surrey Police v PC & Ors* [2024] EWHC 1274 (Fam). The extent to which the

The first mechanism is administrative and is contained within schedule A1 of the Mental Capacity Act 2005, this is the deprivation of liberty safeguards (known as DOLS). DOLS only applies to situations within hospitals and registered care settings, while judicial authorisation can be sought for deprivation of liberty in any setting.[32]

The second mechanism is where the Court of Protection authorises the deprivation of liberty. The court does so using sections 4, 4A and 16 of the Mental Capacity Act 2005. Some judicial authorisations are done using what is described variously as the "streamlined procedure" or the "Re X procedure." Other judicial authorisations are done in the course of a health and welfare case before the Court of Protection.

The "streamlined procedure" is designed to enable a nominated judge of the Court of Protection to be able to authorise the deprivation of liberty which arises from a person's care and support arrangements without a hearing. The procedure follows on from the case of *Re X and others (Deprivation of Liberty).*[33]

Applications to the Court of Protection for orders under section 21A of the Mental Capacity Act 2005 relating to a standard or urgent authorisation under Schedule A1 (DOLS) and applications under s 16(2)(a) to authorise deprivation of liberty under section 4A(3) and (4) pursuant to the streamlined procedure are dealt with by Practice Direction 11A of the Court of Protection Rules 2017.

---

inherent jurisdiction may be used in this way is highly debated and is beyond this work.

32 Equally, the Court of Protection can remove a DOLS authorisation and oversee the deprivation of liberty itself, see for example the decision of HHJ Hilder in *Gloucestershire County Council v AB & Anor* [2022] EWCOP 42

33 [2014] EWCOP 25 (and *No 2* [2014] EWCOP 37)

A Code of Practice was specifically published in respect of DOLS. It is, unfortunately, out of date and caution should be applied when making reference to it.

Specific practice points in respect of high net worth individuals

Deputies

If a deputy for property and affairs is administering a damages award and is making care arrangements for a person which amount to a deprivation of liberty then the deputy must alert the local authority with safeguarding duties for the person to consider those arrangements.

In those circumstances, the deputy (appointed by the court) and the local authority (a public body) will be aware of an unauthorised deprivation of liberty and it will be necessary to apply to the Court of Protection: *SSJ v Staffordshire County Council*[34]. The Court of Appeal in *Staffordshire* did not address who should make the application.

When the case was heard at first instance, Charles J suggested that the obligation lay with the deputy. The general understanding is that, unless damages have been awarded to include the cost of making the application, the local authority should be the applicant. This would accord with their statutory safeguarding duties and would sit with the decision of the Vice President, Theis J, in *Surrey Police v PC & Ors.*[35]

Where a deputy is working with statutory authorities to arrange a person's care and support arrangements, it is likely that any deprivation of liberty arising from those arrangements will be

[34] [2016] EWCA Civ 1317

[35] [2024] EWHC 1274 (Fam)

imputable to the state. That is especially so in circumstances where a public body is funding the care and support arrangements, even if they are not the ultimate decision maker.[36]

The mythos of DOLS

Myths and lore around DOLS are not something which is particular to high net worth individuals. However, it is something which those representing high net worth individuals will need to be aware of, especially if they are unfamiliar with this area of work. DOLS (and court authorisation of deprivations of liberty) are not an authority to detain a person. Rather, it is a process by which restrictions imposed upon them, in their best interests, are authorised.

The recent decision of HHJ Burrows in *Re EM (Deprivation of Liberty, Care Planning & Costs)*[37] is a stark warning that there continues to be significant misunderstanding in this area, even by health, social care and legal professionals. He stated, *inter alia*:

> *51.... the expression "on a dol" or "under a dol", whilst perfectly legitimate abbreviations, must be understood properly and within that context. To be "on" or "under a dol" means to be subject to an order (or authorisation) approving and authorising a care plan which allows the carer to use restrictions that amount to a deprivation of liberty in the best interests of P. Clearly, the emphasis here is on the care plan itself and not the legal status of the restrictions that can be used. The care plan to be used is still a decision to be made by the carer/clinician/MDT in charge on the basis of what they*

36 See the decision of the previous Senior Judge in *Re R* [2016] EWCOP 33

37 [2024] EWCOP 76 (T2)

consider to be needed in the circumstances that arise, and what is in P's best interests.

52. *Unfortunately, when the Court authorises such a care plan that amounts to a "dol" it is seen as being mandatory, like the Court has imposed a prison sentence. That gives rise to an unfortunate misconception on the part of the people who are the subject of these orders that the order, while it remains in place, requires those providing care to keep them actually locked in and locked up.*

53. *In some extreme cases coming before the National DOLs List and the Court of Protection it is easy to see why the misconception arises, particularly when the options for care are all inadequate, P's behaviour is extreme, and LAs are fighting a very difficult and seemingly endless battle to keep P safe.*

54. *However, the principle is always the same. The Court will ask questions like: what is the care plan and how has it been arrived at? What are the risk assessments of alternative plans compared with this one? What does P think? What do other relevant people under s. 4 MCA think? Does the LA/NHS provider (as the case may be) consider the care plan to be the least restrictive option that will address P's needs? What steps are being taken to reduce the need for such an intense care plan? The Court is obliged to scrutinise the answers given.*

Over provision of care and support

In Chapter Four, the costs of care and support were explored. One repeated issue in respect of high net worth individuals is suggestions or arguments that their care provision is simply too high and is unnecessary.

Arguments about over provision of care and support are sometimes grounded in costs but on other occasions arise from a concern that the package which has been devised is not the least restrictive option. The over provision of care and support may well offend against section 1(6) of the Mental Capacity Act 2005.

Again, returning to *Re EM*[38], great heed should be given to what HHJ Burrows said when he stated that it[39], "*is important to remember that the Court is in place to ensure that disputes about capacity, best interests and the proportionality of restrictions are resolved as well as ensuring that there is a consistent scrutiny of a care plan that imposes significant restrictions on P.*"

The use of independent social workers and independent nursing experts can be a helpful tool to ensure that over provision does not occur.

Privately funded residents in care homes

Out of date or not, the DOLS Code of Practice is undoubtedly correct that privately funded residents[40] should benefit from the protection of DOLS. Unfortunately, there remain significant numbers of

38 [2024] EWCOP 76 (T2)

39 Paragraph 58

40 Paragraph 1.21

individuals in care homes (privately funded or not) who do not been assessed in respect of DOLS. The priority tool, published by The Association of Directors of Adult Social Services does not prioritise individuals who are funding their own care. This may lead to the situation that a person is paying for care in a setting in which they do not wish to reside and this has not been scrutinised through the DOLS process.

Home care packages

A person's care and support package, delivered in their own home, may still amount to a deprivation of their liberty[41]. The issue as to whether the deprivation of liberty will be imputable to the state will arise when there is limited or no involvement from public bodies.

Often these arrangements come to the attention of public bodies (in particular, the local authority) as a result of safeguarding concerns. Charles J, at first instance, in *Staffordshire County Council v SRK & Anor*[42] was clear that a local authority should ensure a deprivation of liberty is authorised when revealed during safeguarding enquiries.[43] The Court of Appeal accepted that if the local authority becomes aware of the deprivation of liberty, steps need to be taken to ensure that it is lawful, even if the package is privately funded.[44]

41 The decision of HHJ Hilder in *Re AEL (Mental Capacity Act 2005)* [2021] EWCOP 9 is a helpful example of this.

42 [2016] EWCOP 27

43 See paragraphs 137 – 139 of his judgment

44 See paragraph 72 of *Secretary of State for Justice v Staffordshire County Council & Ors (Rev 1)* [2016] EWCA Civ 1317

Summary

(1) An individual's care and support arrangements will amount to a deprivation of their liberty if they meet the acid test set down in Cheshire West.

(2) A deprivation of liberty may be imputable to the state, even if a public body is not commissioning the care and support.

(3) A deprivation of liberty, for an adult, is primarily authorised by way of Schedule A1 of the Mental Capacity Act 2005 if the adult is accommodated in a registered care setting, or, a hospital.

(4) If an adult is outside of a hospital, or registered care setting, the Court will authorise the deprivation of liberty, either during the course of health and welfare proceedings or following an application using the streamlined procedure.

(5) DOLS is not an authority to detain a person, it is the authorisation of restrictions within their care and support package which are in their best interests.

CHAPTER SEVEN

THE ROLE OF LOCAL AUTHORITIES AND INTEGRATED CARE BOARDS

Introduction

A common feature of health and welfare cases before the Court of Protection is the involvement of at least one public body. In England, the public body involved will most likely be the local authority and/or the relevant Integrated Care Board. In Wales, it will most likely be the local authority and/or the relevant health board. Depending on local commissioning arrangements, there may also be an individual NHS Trust involved in proceedings.

Whilst relatively rare, on occasion, Ministers of State have been parties to Court of Protection proceedings.[45]

An unusual feature of health and welfare cases involving high net worth individuals in the Court of Protection is that often there will not be a public body joined to the proceedings from the outset. The reason for this is simple, often in cases involving high net worth individuals, public bodies have had little or no involvement with the person ahead of the proceedings being issued. This can sometimes pose problems for the court in resolving the issues before it and is addressed in more detail below.

---

45 See for example *The Secretary of State for the Home Department v Skripal* [2018] EWCOP 6

The local authority

At the time of writing there are 317 local authorities in England. There are, broadly speaking, five different types: (i) county councils; (ii) district councils; (iii) unitary authorities; (iv) metropolitan districts and (v) London Boroughs. Functions will differ depending on the type of local authority.

At the time of writing there are 22 unitary county and county borough councils in Wales.

For the purposes of health and welfare proceedings, the most important statutory duties are in respect of an individual's care and support. Additionally, the Court of Protection will consider the steps taken by local authorities in respect of their duty to safeguard individuals from abuse and neglect. In some cases, other local authority functions may be in issue, with people under the age of 25 issues as to education arise.[46] Questions as to housing duties and environmental health duties sometimes arise in other cases.

Care and support: England

In England, the Care Act 2014 sets out a local authorities' duties when assessing a person's care and support needs. The Care Act contains general legal duties that local authorities have towards each individual living in their local jurisdiction. This is regardless of whether they have needs for care and support, eligible needs, or neither. These general duties apply regardless of how long individuals have been living in the local area for.

---

[46] See for example the decision of HHJ Dodds in *Local Authority v GP (Capacity – Care, Support and Education)* [2020] EWCOP 56

Whilst many of the local authority's care and support duties relate to the entire population of an area (for example, in relation to promoting individual wellbeing), specific duties in respect of the provision of care and support needs only apply to an individual who is ordinarily resident in that area.

The first role of the local authority in respect of care and support, is assessing what those needs are. Thereafter the local authority will establish if the assessed needs meet the national eligibility threshold, in doing so they will apply The Care and Support (Eligibility Criteria) Regulations 2015. A care and support plan will be compiled to meet the person's eligible care and support needs.

A financial assessment will be conducted to determine how much, if anything, a person needs to contribute towards the cost of their care to meet their assessed eligible needs.

Care and support: Wales

In Wales, the Social Services and Well-being (Wales) Act 2014 provides a comparable framework for people with care and support needs. As with the English framework, a financial assessment will be conducted to determine how much a person needs to contribute to the cost of their care.

Safeguarding

In both England and Wales, local authorities have safeguarding duties. In England, the principal safeguarding duties in respect of adults are found within section 42 of the Care Act 2014. In Wales, the safeguarding duty primarily arises from section 126 of the Social Services and Well-being (Wales) Act 2014.

Again, whilst the English and Welsh system is comparable, the Welsh system is arguably stronger. In Wales, aside from safeguarding duties, there is also the ability to apply for an "an adult protection and support order" under section 127 of the Social Services and Well-being (Wales) Act 2014. These orders are granted by the Magistrates' Court and provide a power of entry, and to speak to an individual alone, when there is a concern that there is a risk of abuse and/or neglect.

The Integrated Care Boards

At the time of writing, there are 42 Integrated Care Boards in England. Each ICB has its own constitution and geographical area of responsibility. The Integrated Care Board (ICB) is a statutory body responsible for local NHS services, functions, performance and budgets. It is directly accountable to the NHS and is made up of local NHS trusts, primary care providers, and local authorities.

Health Boards

In Wales, there are 7 Health Boards at present. Each Health Board is responsible for planning, commissioning and providing local healthcare services to address local needs

How public bodies come to be part of health and welfare proceedings before the Court of Protection

Frequently, it will be a public body who initiates health and welfare proceedings before the Court of Protection. Primarily, the public body will be commissioning care, support or treatment provision which in some respect is being disputed. Alternatively, a local authority may be bringing proceedings due to a safeguarding concern.

However, it is not uncommon for health and welfare proceedings involving high net worth individuals to have no public body involvement at the outset of proceedings. They can become involved in a variety of different ways which are outlined below:

Third party disclosure orders

Section 47(1) of the Mental Capacity Act 2005 gives the Court of Protection the same powers, rights, privileges and authority as the High Court. The Court of Protection may make orders against public bodies for the disclosure of documents in their possession. The court will not do so unless it is likely to assist in the determination of the issues before the court. Nor will the court make broad, unspecified orders for disclosure.

Section 49 orders

Section 49(3) of the Mental Capacity Act 2005 empowers the Court of Protection to call for a report from a local authority or NHS body. The court may ask either body to conduct a capacity assessment in respect of a particular issue, or to report on some aspect of an individual's care or treatment.

An NHS body takes its definition from section 49(10) of the Mental Capacity Act 2005 and section 148 of the Health and Social Care (Community Health and Standards) Act 2003. The definition of NHS body in section 148 does not include GP practices. Therefore, GP practices cannot be directly ordered by the Court of Protection to produce a report under section 49.

In 2022, a meeting took place between the previous Vice President of the Court of Protection (Hayden J) and the Senior Judge (HHJ Hilder) with various NHS Directors. As a result of that meeting, a letter was published by the previous Vice President outlining the approach to the use of these orders. Hayden J stated, amongst other things:

> *Instructions under Section 49 should be clearly focused with tight identification of the issues. It should be expected that the reports will be concise and will not require extensive analysis across a wider range of questions than those contemplated in the Practice Direction. Reports requiring that kind of response should be addressed to an independent expert.*

Joinder

A public body will not be automatically joined as a party to proceedings, even if the application before the Court of Protection reveals serious safeguarding concerns.

The Court of Protection Rules 2017, rule 9.13(2) permits the court to join a public body as a party if it considers that it is desirable to do so for the purpose of dealing with the application.

Specific practice points in respect of high net worth individuals

Financial eligibility and safeguarding

A concerning recent trend has been for some local authorities in England to exclude individuals from safeguarding processes because they are either: (i) not receiving care and support commissioned by the local authority or (ii) would not be financially eligible to have their care and support needs met by the local authority. This is a fundamental misunderstanding as to how section 42 of the Care Act 2014 operates. It is unclear where this misunderstanding comes from but it leaves high net worth individuals without a key protection provided by the Care Act 2014.

If health and welfare proceedings are underway in respect of high net worth individuals and this issue arises, the Court of Protection will often join the local authority as a party to proceedings to explain their stance. There is no published judgment which grapples with this point but it is foreseeable that a consistent failure to fulfil statutory duties may result in declarations and costs awards being made against a public body.[47]

A refusal, or resistance, to section 49 reports

As indicated above, it is not uncommon for high net worth individuals to be unknown to local NHS services. When section 49 reports are made against local services who do not know the individual concerned, they will often seek to discharge the order, or to vary it.

In the circumstances, the court is faced with determining what approach to take. Ultimately, the court may have no choice but to discharge the section 49 order if it will cause an unnecessary delay in proceedings, or, if the body the order is made against does not have a report writer with the necessary expertise.

It may be that the order is directed at a different public body or an order is made against the Public Guardian for the appointment of a Special Visitor. In some cases, it is determined that the best approach is to instruct, and pay, an independent expert.

---

[47] See, for example, the approach of Keehan J in *ND (Court of Protection: Costs and Declarations)* [2020] EWCOP 42

Summary

(1) It is not unusual for high net worth individuals to be unknown to local statutory services. This does not prevent those local statutory services from becoming involved in Court of Protection proceedings.

(2) A local authority will not be automatically joined to health and welfare proceedings relating to a high net worth individual, even if there are significant safeguarding concerns. The court may join a public body if the test in rule 9.13(2) is met.

(3) Statutory services may become involved in proceedings by way of section 49 reports. The use of section 49 reports can, sometimes, be contentious and alternatives may need to be found, for example, independent experts or by the appointment of a Special Visitor.

CHAPTER EIGHT

PREDATORY MARRIAGES, RELATIONSHIPS AND FRIENDSHIPS

Introduction

Predatory marriage is a phenomenon that has been discussed in Parliament and in the media, there are growing concerns in respect of adults who may be vulnerable to it.

The Law Commission started the process of consulting on reforming the law of wills in 2017. A Supplementary Consultation Paper was released in on 5 October 2023 this included two topics: possible reforms to enable electronic wills and to the rule that a marriage or civil partnership revokes a will. The supplementary consultation period closed on 8 December 2023.

The consultation in respect of the rule that a marriage or civil partnership revokes a will was due to concerns in respect of predatory marriage. The Law Commission will publish their final Report and a draft Bill containing their recommendations in early 2025. Meanwhile, parliamentarians are discussing the relationship between predatory marriage and the use of lasting powers of attorney.

Predatory marriage is not the only source of concern. The other issue which is increasingly causing concern to safeguarding professionals, the police and courts are cases where an offender befriends a person with vulnerabilities with the intention of then exploiting them financially, physically or sexually. This is sometimes described as, "mate crime."

Concerns as to the true nature of a relationship are sometimes the focus of health and welfare proceedings in the Court of Protection. Concerns as to financial exploitation are something which features in cases involving high net worth individuals.

Mental capacity and relationships

As with any other decision, the law assumes that an adult has the mental capacity to make a decision as to their relationships until it is proved otherwise. Mental capacity assessments in this area remain legally challenging.

Marriage

At present, the law approaches assessing a person's capacity to marry as being relating to the act of marriage, rather than specific to the people who are to be married. Whether the marriage is wise or not, is, according to the caselaw, irrelevant.[48] The courts have stated that the bar as to capacity in this regard must not be set too high so as to avoid discrimination.

When assessing a person's capacity to marry, the relevant information in respect of that decision has been said to be:

(a) The broad nature of the marriage contract;

(b) The duties and responsibilities that normally attach to marriage, including that there may be financial consequences

48 See decision of Hedley J in *A, B and C v X and Z* [2012] EWHC 2400 (COP) at paragraph 32.

and that spouses have a particular status and connection with regard to each other;

(c) That the essence of marriage is for two people to live together and to love one another;

(d) That marriage will make any existing will invalid.

There remains a debate as to whether a person must have the capacity to engage in sexual relations for them to have capacity to marry.

Sex

Capacity to make decisions as to sex has been considered by the Supreme Court.[49] In doing so, the Supreme Court moved away from the language of somebody having the mental capacity to, "consent to sex" to whether they have the mental capacity to, "engage in sex."

When assessing a person's capacity to engage in sex, the relevant information in respect of that decision has been said to be:

(a) the sexual nature and character of the act of sexual intercourse, including the mechanics of the act;

(b) the fact that the other person must have the ability to consent to the sexual activity and must in fact consent before and throughout the sexual activity;

(c) the fact that P can say yes or no to having sexual relations and is able to decide whether to give or withhold consent;

[49] *A Local Authority v JB* [2021] UKSC 52

(d) that a reasonably foreseeable consequence of sexual intercourse between a man and woman is that the woman will become pregnant;

(e) that there are health risks involved, particularly the acquisition of sexually transmitted and transmissible infections, and that the risk of sexually transmitted infection can be reduced by the taking of precautions such as the use of a condom.

Contact

The terminology in respect of relationships (beyond marriage and sex) are generally encapsulated in the term, "contact." That terminology covers a broad spectrum of relationships, from meeting a stranger to spending time with a loved one.

Three approaches have been taken to assessing a person's mental capacity to make decisions as to contact with other people:

(i) Contact with a specific person;

(ii) Contact with categories of people;

(iii) Contact with others generally.

The Official Solicitor has, historically, had concerns about person specific capacity assessments but has, in some cases, concluded that is the correct approach. Social workers (and other assessors) often struggle with assessing capacity to make decisions as to contact in a way that is not specific to a person. However, it is sometimes impractical to conduct multiple assessments in respect of a variety of different people and the use of categories[50] solves difficulties in this regard,

Whichever approach is taken, the relevant information is usually formulated from the judgment of Theis J in *LBX v K, L and M*[51]:

(a) Who the contact will be with;

(b) In broad terms, the nature of the relationship between the person under assessment and the contact in question;

(c) If there is a specific person or people in respect of whom decisions about contact need to be made, what sort of contact the person under assessment could have with each of the individuals with whom they may have contact;

(d) The positive or negative aspects of having contact with each person;

(e) Whether the person with whom contact is being considered has previous criminal convictions or poses a risk to the protected party;

(f) The risks of having unfettered contact with people generally;

(g) Where the proposed contact is with a family member, what a family relationship is and that it is in a different category to other categories of contact.

---

50 See the judgment in *Re EOA* [2021] EWCOP 20 where three different categories of person on the facts of the case were utilised.

51 [2013] EWHC 3230 (Fam)

Managing risks from a relationship

Section 27(1) of the Mental Capacity Act 2005

If a person lacks the mental capacity to engage in sexual relations, or lacks the capacity to marry, then the Court of Protection cannot intercede and make a best interests decision in this regard. The court cannot consent on a person's behalf to them having sex, or, make a best interests decision for them to marry: section 27(1) of the Mental Capacity Act 2005.

Contact restrictions

Generally, concerns in respect of relationships are managed by way of contact restrictions. Such restrictions will likely engage both parties' rights under Article 8 of the European Convention on Human Rights and needs to be carefully managed.

Some contact restrictions will be managed by the Court of Protection and can be enforced by the court using a penal notice if necessary. It will, potentially, be a contempt of court if a person breaches an injunctive provision.

Injunctions

In *Re G (Court of Protection: Injunction)*[52], the Court of Appeal grappled with the approach to be taken in respect of injunctions made by the Court of Protection. Paragraph 82 of the decision is helpful in setting out the legal framework:

---

52 [2022] EWCA Civ 1312

82. The Court of Protection does have power to grant injunctions under s.16(5) of the 2005 Act, both in the case where a deputy has been appointed under s.16(2)(b) and in the case where the Court has made an order taking a decision for P under s.16(2)(a). In doing so, it is exercising the power conferred on it by s.47(1) and such an injunction can therefore only be granted when it is just and convenient to do so. This requirement is now to be understood in line with the majority judgment in Broad Idea as being satisfied where there is an interest which merits protection and a legal or equitable principle which justifies exercising the power to order the defendant to do or not do something.

Specific practice points in respect of high net worth individuals: the decision in *Re BU* [2021] EWCOP54

BU was a 70-year-old woman who had vascular dementia. The judgment details that she had assets in excess of £1.3 million.

In 2016 she struck up a friendship with a man, NC, who had previous multiple convictions for fraud, theft, blackmail and firearm offences, some of which had resulted in custodial sentences. The argument of BU's family was that, over time, NC had exerted increasing control and influence over BU's personal life and finances. This included: transferring cash, a boat, a caravan, a pick-up truck and a van to him.

By the time the matter came before Roberts J, final declarations had been made that BU lacked capacity to make decisions in relation to her property and financial affairs, and a deputy was appointed to manage her property and affairs. The purpose of the deputy was to protect BU's finances from any ongoing risk of exploitation.

BU's daughter sought from the Court of Protection a declaration that her mother lacked capacity to make decisions about her contact with others, including NC; an order preventing NC from having further contact with BU (and the continuation of an injunction to this end which had already provided for this for over a year); and an order under the court's inherent jurisdiction which prevented a marriage or civil partnership between NC and BU or, alternatively, an order pursuant to section 63A of the Family Law Act 1996 (a forced marriage protection order).

As Roberts J reminded herself at the outset of her judgment (in paragraph 2), "[i]*n circumstances where personal autonomy and life choices are a central aspect of the human rights which this court is bound to uphold and respect, it is only in limited circumstances where it can or should intervene.*"

Having heard the evidence, Roberts J had to determine what steps to take to avoid any further risk which might be posed by NC to BU. She stated at paragraph 98 of her judgment:

> *In these circumstances it is agreed that the options for the court in relation to contact between BU and NC are binary: either it will sanction ongoing contact or it will not. There is no option or facility for supervised contact at this stage. Taking into account all the relevant circumstances in section 4(2) and BU's expressed wishes and feelings as I am obliged to do pursuant to section 4(6) of the 2005 Act, I am in no doubt at all that it is not in her best interests to be exposed to further risk of financial abuse and/or the risk of future manipulation by NC through the control he has exerted through his behaviour to date. I regard it as essential that steps are taken at the earliest opportunity to address and reverse the current estrangement between BU and her family and this is unlikely to happen whilst NC's corrosive influence over her persists. The immediate need is for BU to receive therapeutic*

assistance in coming to terms with the loss of this relationship and the reasons why that step through court intervention has been necessary. If a view is subsequently taken that this position needs to be reviewed at a later stage once BU has had an opportunity to engage in therapy, the court can look again at the matter. It will remain to be seen whether NC remains interested in contact with her at that stage and/or whether he will be prepared at that stage to undertake whatever therapy or other work is required of him in order to address his own behaviour.

Due to the facts and history of the case, Roberts J concluded that there remained a risk of NC marrying BU. As a result, she made an injunction which prevented NC from entering, or attempting to enter, a civil partnership with BU without first obtaining specific permission from the court. In relation to marriage, she followed *Re K (Secretary of State for Justice and another intervening)*[53], she made a forced marriage protection order.

Summary

(1) Predatory marriage and exploitative relationships are an increased area of concern. The Law Commission is currently considering whether predatory marriages may be discouraged by removing the automatic revocation of a will upon marriage.

(2) The mental capacity to marry is not concerned with the wisdom of the marriage.

(3) The Mental Capacity Act 2005 cannot be used to consent to a person engaging in sex or getting married.

53 [2020] EWCA Civ 190

(4) Injunctions can be used to prevent contact in a concerning relationship, other provisions might be appropriate, including forced marriage protection orders.

CHAPTER NINE

THE BREAKDOWN OF RELATIONSHIPS IN HIGH NET WORTH FAMILIES

Introduction

The breakdown of relationships in high net worth families is often the starting point of a health and welfare case in the Court of Protection. Sometimes it is the parents of a disabled adult child who divorce. On other occasions, it is the adult children of an elderly person; the relationship between siblings can become fraught, especially in circumstances if one of the siblings is organising the care arrangements.

The Mental Capacity Act 2005 does not contain any expectation that a parent and child will have contact. Some parents struggle with the idea that when their disabled child becomes an adult they will no longer have the ability to make decisions on their behalf. There is no equivalent of parental responsibility, there are no child arrangements orders.

Equally, the Mental Capacity Act 2005 contains no presumption that a person will continue to live in their own home, or that they will continue to have contact with all family members should they lose capacity to make decisions for themselves at a certain point.

The basic concept of best interests decision making around where somebody lives

Often, the most contentious issue in the breakdown of relationships in high net worth families is where the person who lacks capacity around their residence ends up living. Elsewhere in this book, other best interests decisions are explored. Each time a best interests decision is made it will follow the best interests checklist in section 4 of the Mental Capacity Act 2005.

Having established that a person lacks the mental capacity to make decisions as to their residence, it should be clear what the available options are. If it is not clear, a proper appraisal of where the person might be able to live ought to be done before the best interests analysis is embarked upon.

As said elsewhere in this book, it should not be presumed that a person is unable to live in their own home, especially if funds are available to make necessary adaptations. Equally, as highlighted above, it should not be assumed that living with a family member is the only available option for a person.

Having established the available options, it is important to try and establish the person's wishes and feelings with regard to where they wish to live. This might, in some cases, involve using a speech and language therapist, or an advocate, or somebody independent from the family if there is a dispute. In contentious circumstances, the court may well be cautious about other family members stating what the person's wishes and feelings are. The decision maker, and the court, will likely give significant weight to the person's wishes and feelings.

The decision maker, and ultimately the court, will also give significant weight to a person's past wishes and feelings, if evidenced, in respect of where they wish to live. There may be documents where they have set out an intention to live with a particular family member. Those documents do not need to be formally drafted but again, if there is a dispute, it is likely that the veracity of the documents may be challenged.

If it is practicable and appropriate, the decision maker will consult with others under section 4(7) of the Mental Capacity Act 2005, again, if family members are in dispute as to where the person ought to live, this may be a relatively difficult or limited exercise. More helpful may be the views of others engaged in caring for the person or interested in their welfare, this might include, for example carers or medical professionals.

Section 4(11) of the Mental Capacity Act 2005 also means that the decision maker should consider the relevant circumstances relating to the decision. In respect of where a person lives, that might include things such as:

(i) The cost of the available options, how long they can afford to live there;

(ii) To what extent are the options adapted to meet the person's individual needs;

(iii) If there are staff at the options, their experience and ability to meet the person's needs;

(iv) Whether the person will be living alone and what their social opportunities will be;

(v) For some people, whether they are able to have pets live with them at a particular option might be important.

The words of Peter Jackson J (as he then was) in *Re M (Best Interests: Deprivation of Liberty)*[54] are an important reminder of the type of issues which arise when deciding where a person lives:

> 38 *In the end, if M remains confined in a home she is entitled to ask "What for?" The only answer that could be provided at the moment is "To keep you alive as long as possible." In my view that is not a sufficient answer. The right to life and the state's obligation to protect it is not absolute and the court must surely have regard to the person's own assessment of her quality of life. In M's case there is little to be said for a solution that attempts, without any guarantee of success, to preserve for her a daily life without meaning or happiness and which she, with some justification, regards as insupportable.*

The basic concept of best interests decision making around contact decisions

The previous chapter addressed how to assess a person's capacity in respect of contact and dealt with those cases where the court has had to take steps to prevent contact between people.

The majority of cases involving contact decisions will not require injunctive provisions, rather the court will be invited to approve some form of contact schedule. From the outset, it is important to note that the court will not force a person to have contact with someone when they do not want to have it.

54 [2013] EWCOP 3456

The court will likely take the approach of establishing parameters for the contact whilst being clear that it will be led by the person's wishes and feelings at the material time when contact is due to take place.

However, the court will, on occasion, step in and prevent contact from taking place even in circumstances when a person wants it. Article 8 of the European Convention on Human Rights contains no explicit procedural requirements in this regard but the decision-making process must be fair.[55]

Specific practice points in respect of high net worth individuals

Moving abroad

Sometimes high net worth families want to move their incapacitous family member abroad. The decision in *Re UR*[56] is particularly helpful in this regard. At paragraph 57 of the judgment, Hayden J endorsed a checklist in respect of information which would need to be obtained for the court to consider a permanent move abroad:

> *i. Liaison with the relevant Embassy/ Consulate (in the first instance) to ascertain what guidance and assistance can be provided;*
>
> *ii. Evidence as to physical health to travel (GP);*
>
> *iii. Evidence as to mental health to travel (psychiatrist);*

---

[55] See for example *AN v Lithuania* [2016] ECHR 462

[56] [2021] EWCOP 10

iv. Legal opinion regarding citizenship, benefit entitlement, health and social care provision in the relevant country, and such other issues relevant to the case;

v. Consideration of any applications that need to be made as a consequence of any legal opinion provided;

vi. Independent social work evidence regarding the viability of the proposed package of care in the relevant country if such evidence cannot be provided by the parties to the proceedings or a direction under section 49 MCA;

vii. Confirmation of travel costings from the commissioners of the care package, both in relation to P and any carers that may need to travel with them (who will pay?);

viii. Confirmation that the necessary medication/ care will be available during travel from the UK/ for the immediate future in the new country

ix. Transition plan/ care plan, to include a contingency plan and how the matter should return to court in the event of an emergency in implementing the proposed plan;

x. Best interest evidence from the relevant commissioners;

xi. Wishes and feelings evidence;

xii. Residual orders to allow the plan to be implemented, including single issue financial orders regarding opening/closing of UK bank accounts, the purchasing of essential items to travel (if necessary);

xiii. Covid-19 considerations prior to travel (if applicable)

Family / Parenting Coordinators

In some cases, especially those involving a breakdown of relationship between parents of a disabled adult child, it is suggested that contact arrangements will likely be best managed by the use of a family or parenting coordinator. Such a suggestion is, superficially, attractive, especially if the professional has been involved ahead of the Court of Protection proceedings. The difficulty in this regard is that these professionals are primarily used in the context of private children's law proceedings, not, giving effect to orders of the Court of Protection. Sometimes independent social workers have been used an alternative.

Passports and foreign travel

Public bodies do not have the lawful authority to seize the passport of an individual who is unable to make certain decisions for themselves. Despite this, in a number of cases, local authorities have taken a person's passport due to concerns that a family member may take them out of the country.

The Court of Protection does not make passport orders. However, if a person lacks the mental capacity to make decisions in respect of foreign travel, or applying for a passport, then the Court of Protection may make orders in this regard.[57]

[57] See for example *Re EOA* [2021] EWCOP 20

Summary

(1) The Mental Capacity Act 2005 does not contain the same expectations as to parental contact, or involvement, as the Children Act 1989.

(2) The Court of Protection will give significant weight to a person's wishes and feelings but is not bound to follow them, rather it will apply all of the factors in section 4 of the Mental Capacity Act 2005.

(3) The Court of Protection can determine that someone ought to move overseas and will likely apply the checklist contained in *Re UR* before making that decision. Whilst the Court of Protection does not make passport orders, it may follow the approach in *Re EOA* in respect of a person who lacks the mental capacity to make decisions as to foreign travel.

CHAPTER TEN

COSTS IN HEALTH AND WELFARE PROCEEDINGS BEFORE THE COURT OF PROTECTION

Introduction

The usual rule in health and welfare proceedings is that the parties pay their own costs of the proceedings. However, this rule is rebuttable. It is not uncommon for applications to be made in circumstances where public bodies have erroneously refused to take steps in respect of a high net worth individual, or where a family member has had to step in and bring an application that usually would have been brought by a local authority under their safeguarding duties.

Legal Framework

The Court of Protection Rules

The general rule in welfare cases is that there should be no order as to costs: Rule 19.3 of the Court of Protection Rules[58] provides:

> *'Where the proceedings concern P's personal welfare the general rule is that there will be no order as to the costs of the proceedings*

[58] Made pursuant to sections 55 and 56 of the Mental Capacity Act 2005

> *or of that part of the proceedings that concerns P's personal welfare'*

Rule 19.5 of the Court of Protection Rules 2017 makes plain that the court may depart from the general rules about costs and in particular may do so having regard to the conduct of any public authority.

The court may depart from the general rule on costs in either welfare or property and affairs cases: the relevant factors are set out at Rule 19.5:

> ***Departing from the general rule***
>
> *19.5.—*
>
> *(1) The court may depart from rules 19.2 to 19.4 if the circumstances so justify, and in deciding whether departure is justified the court will have regard to all the circumstances, including–*
>
> *(a) the conduct of the parties;*
>
> *(b) whether a party has succeeded on part of his case, even if he has not been wholly successful; and*
>
> *(c) the role of any public body involved in the proceedings.*
>
> *(2) The conduct of the parties includes–*
>
> *(a) conduct before, as well as during, the proceedings;*
>
> *(b) whether it was reasonable for a party to raise, pursue or contest a particular issue;*

> (c) *the manner in which a party has made or responded to an application or a particular issue;*
>
> (d) *whether a party who has succeeded in his application or response to an application, in whole or in part, exaggerated any matter contained in his application or response; and*
>
> (e) *any failure by a party to comply with a rule, practice direction or court order*

Previous decisions of the Court of Protection

The previous decisions of the Court of Protection do not generally give guidance but are instead, *"useful examples of the manner in which the court has exercised its powers"* (*London Borough of Hillingdon v Neary & Ors* [2011] EWHC 3522 (COP) Peter Jackson J); and he echoed this comment in *VA & Ors v Hertfordshire Partnership NHS Foundation Trust & Ors* [2011] EWHC 3524 (COP) where he stated that each application must be considered on its own merits.

In *Neary* (supra) Peter Jackson J (as he then was) said at paragraph 9 the court's process was in two stages:

a. Is a departure from the general rule justified?

b. If so, what order should be made?

Bad faith or flagrant misconduct are not conditions precedent to justify a departure from the normal principle. In *Re M* [2015] EWCOP 45 it was suggested by Baker J (as he then was) at paragraph 6 that a costs award might be appropriate where one party *"has been found [guilty] of .... conduct that can be described as 'significantly unreasonable."*

Examples of cases where costs awards have been made are:

a. *G v E (Costs)* [2010] EWHC 3385 (Fam): Baker J ordered the local authority to pay the costs of the other parties, including pre-litigation costs, some on an indemnity basis (to be subject to detailed assessment if not agreed), due its failure to comply with its obligations under the MCA and the Convention.

b. *London Borough of Hillingdon v Neary & Ors* (supra): unlawful removal of P, failure to carry out proper assessments or consultation, delay in bringing proceedings in the Court of Protection.

c. *VA & Ors v Hertfordshire Partnership NHS Foundation Trust & Ors* (supra): failure to follow the MCA and Code of Practice before proceedings were launched.

d. *North Somerset Council v LW & Ors* [2014] EWCOP 3: Keehan J ordered the Trust to pay the Official Solicitor's full costs of an obstetric case for two days. Planning was inadequate, and costs had been wasted by a failure to carry out an urgent assessment of capacity.

e. *Somerset County Council v MK & Anor* [2015] EWCOP B1: full costs on an indemnity basis were awarded where the Local Authority had carried out a *"manifestly bungled investigation"* which led to the (unnecessary) proceedings, compounded by, *"unreasonable conduct during the course of proceedings"* which lengthened and complicated the final hearing.

f. *MR v SR & Bury Clinical Commissioning Group* [2016] EWCOP 54: Hayden J directed the CCG to pay the costs of the applicant daughter of P, who had ultimately been compelled to issue proceedings for withdrawal of CANH in order to resolve the dispute.

g. *LB of Redbridge v A, B and E (Failure to Comply with Directions)* [2016] EWHC 2627 (Fam): MacDonald J ordered a local authority to show cause why it should not pay the wasted costs of the ineffective hearings.

h. *London Borough of Lambeth v MCS & Anor* [2018] EWCOP 20: Newton J awarded the whole of the costs of the proceedings against the public authorities where attempts to find an alternative placement had *been "ineffectual … order after order was not complied with … what is impossible to ignore is the disorganised thinking, planning and management."* An award was made against the local authority and CCG 'jointly and severally'.

i. *Re ND (Court of Protection: Costs and Declarations)* [2020] EWCOP 42: Keehan J made a costs order against the local authority in favour of the Official Solicitor for two wasted hearings due (inter alia) the disorganised thinking and planning of the local authority.

j. *Re JB (Costs)* [2020] EWCOP 49: Keehan J ordered the Local Authority to pay the costs of SB (a family member) and the Official Solicitor occasioned by an application for an injunction.

Where the court is satisfied that it is appropriate to depart from the usual rule, the courts have demonstrated resistance to detailed arguments about who should pay for precisely what, approving instead a "broad brush" approach (*Manchester City Council v G & Ors* [2011] EWCA Civ 939 at [25].

Similarly, in *Neary* (supra), Peter Jackson J rejected the approach (argued for by both parties) of breaking down the proceedings into stages, saying that the court was not constrained by how the parties framed the arguments and that he preferred to look at the matter as a whole, saying that he favoured "an approach that was as simple as possible".

In *MR v SR & Bury Clinical Commissioning Group* (supra), Hayden J described the determination of costs as not a precise science, but "an intuitive art reflecting the Judge's feel for the litigation as a whole."

Recently, in *Cardiff and Vale University Health Board v NN* [2024] EWCOP 61, Victoria Butler-Cole KC, sitting as a Tier 3 judge of the Court of Protection, made a costs order against the applicant, Health Board. In doing so, she differentiated between their conduct at different stages of the proceedings and made adverse costs awards accordingly.

Summary

(1) The usual rule in health and welfare cases is for parties to pay their own costs, the court may disapply this rule due to a party's conduct both before and during the proceedings.

(2) Bad faith or flagrant misconduct are not conditions precedent to justify a departure from the normal principle.

(3) The court is unlikely to take a mechanical approach to determining whether to disapply the usual rule, rather a costs award will reflect the judge's feel for the litigation.

MORE BOOKS BY LAW BRIEF PUBLISHING

A selection of our other titles available now:-

'A Practical Guide to Probation Breaches and Other Applications' by Mark Thomas
'A Practical Guide to Remarriage and Divorce' by Cordelia Williams & Claire Howard
'A Practical Guide to Privacy, Transparency, Reporting Restrictions and Closed Proceedings in the Court of Protection' by Laura Mannering
'Beaumont on Barristers – A Guide to Defending Disciplinary Proceedings (Second Edition)' by Marc Beaumont
'A Practical Guide to Payments for Environmental Services' by Ben Sharples
'A Practical Guide to the Law of Pregnancy and Maternity at Work' by Rebecca Thomas
'A Practical Guide to Redundancy – Second Edition' by Philip Hyland & Collette Moore
'A Practical Guide to International Issues for Scottish Family Lawyers' by Susie Mountain, Donna McKay, Ken MacDonald
'A Practical Guide to the Law on Deprivation of Liberty' by Ben Troke
'A Practical Guide to Rights over Airspace and Subsoil – Second Edition' by Daniel Gatty
'A Practical Guide to the Law in Relation to Inquests' by Ramya Nagesh
'A Practical Guide to the Construction and Rectification of Wills and Trust Instruments (Second Edition)' by Edward Hewitt
'A Practical Guide to Data Protection in Social Housing' by Clare Paterson
'A Practical Guide to Spousal Maintenance – Second Edition' by Liz Cowell
'A Practical Guide to International Parental Child Abduction Law (England and Wales)' by Dr Onyója Momoh
'A Practical Guide to Deprivation of British Citizenship' by Sean Ell
'A Practical Guide to Commercial Property Service Charges' by Rachel Garton
'A Practical Guide to Clinical Negligence – Third Edition' by Geoffrey Simpson-Scott (Geoff)
'A Practical Guide to the Rights of Grandparents in Children Proceedings – Second Edition' by Stuart Barlow

'The Electronic Communications Code: A Practical Guide – Second Edition' by Kerry Bretherton KC, James Castle, Mark Loveday
'A Practical Guide to the Independent School Standards – September 2023 Edition' by Sarah McKimm
'A Practical Guide to Estate Administration and Crypto Assets' by Richard Marshall
'A Practical Guide to Parental Alienation in Private and Public Law Children Cases' by Sam King QC & Frankie Shama
'Contested Heritage – Removing Art from Land and Historic Buildings' by Richard Harwood QC, Catherine Dobson, David Sawtell
'The Limits of Separate Legal Personality: When Those Running a Company Can Be Held Personally Liable for Losses Caused to Third Parties Outside of the Company' by Dr Mike Wilkinson
'A Practical Guide to Transgender Law' by Robin Moira White & Nicola Newbegin
'A Practical Guide to 'Stranded Spouses' in Family Law' by Mani Singh Basi
'A Practical Guide to Residential Freehold Conveyancing' by Lorraine Richardson
'A Practical Guide to Pensions on Divorce for Lawyers' by Bryan Scant
'A Practical Guide to Challenging Sham Marriage Allegations in Immigration Law' by Priya Solanki
'A Practical Guide to Digital Communications Evidence in Criminal Law' by Sam Willis
'A Practical Guide to Legal Rights in Scotland' by Sarah-Jane Macdonald
'A Practical Guide to New Build Conveyancing' by Paul Sams & Rebecca East
'A Practical Guide to Inherited Wealth on Divorce' by Hayley Trim
'A Practical Guide to Practice Direction 12J and Domestic Abuse in Private Law Children Proceedings' by Rebecca Cross & Malvika Jaganmohan
'A Practical Guide to Confiscation and Restraint' by Narita Bahra QC, John Carl Townsend, David Winch
'A Practical Guide to the Law of Forests in Scotland' by Philip Buchan
'A Practical Guide to Health and Medical Cases in Immigration Law' by Rebecca Chapman & Miranda Butler
'A Practical Guide to Bad Character Evidence for Criminal Practitioners by Aparna Rao
'A Practical Guide to Extradition Law post-Brexit' by Myles Grandison et al
'A Practical Guide to Hoarding and Mental Health for Housing Lawyers' by Rachel Coyle

'Stephens on Contractual Indemnities' by Richard Stephens
'A Practical Guide to the EU Succession Regulation' by Richard Frimston
'A Practical Guide to Solicitor and Client Costs – Second Edition' by Robin Dunne
'Constructive Dismissal – Practice Pointers and Principles' by Benjimin Burgher
'A Practical Guide to Religion and Belief Discrimination Claims in the Workplace' by Kashif Ali
'A Practical Guide to the Law of Medical Treatment Decisions' by Ben Troke
'Fundamental Dishonesty and QOCS in Personal Injury Proceedings: Law and Practice' by Jake Rowley
'A Practical Guide to the Law in Relation to School Exclusions' by Charlotte Hadfield & Alice de Coverley
'A Practical Guide to Divorce for the Silver Separators' by Karin Walker
'The Right to be Forgotten – The Law and Practical Issues' by Melissa Stock
'A Practical Guide to Planning Law and Rights of Way in National Parks, the Broads and AONBs' by James Maurici QC, James Neill et al
'A Practical Guide to Election Law' by Tom Tabori
'A Practical Guide to the Law in Relation to Surrogacy' by Andrew Powell
'A Practical Guide to Claims Arising from Fatal Accidents – Second Edition' by James Patience
'A Practical Guide to Asbestos Claims' by Jonathan Owen & Gareth McAloon
'A Practical Guide to Stamp Duty Land Tax in England and Northern Ireland' by Suzanne O'Hara
'A Practical Guide to the Law of Farming Partnerships' by Philip Whitcomb
'A Practical Guide to the Law of Unlawful Eviction and Harassment – Second Edition' by Stephanie Lovegrove
'A Practical Guide to Costs in Personal Injury Claims – Second Edition' by Matthew Hoe
'A Practical Guide to the General Data Protection Regulation (GDPR) – Second Edition' by Keith Markham
'A Practical Guide to Working with Litigants in Person and McKenzie Friends in Family Cases' by Stuart Barlow
'Protecting Unregistered Brands: A Practical Guide to the Law of Passing Off' by Lorna Brazell
'A Practical Guide to Secondary Liability and Joint Enterprise Post-Jogee' by Joanne Cecil & James Mehigan

'A Practical Guide to the Pre-Action RTA Claims Protocol for Personal Injury Lawyers' by Antonia Ford

'A Practical Guide to Neighbour Disputes and the Law' by Alexander Walsh

'A Practical Guide to Coercive Control for Legal Practitioners and Victims' by Rachel Horman

'A Practical Guide to the Law of Driverless Cars – Second Edition'

by Alex Glassbrook, Emma Northey & Scarlett Milligan

'A Practical Guide to TOLATA Claims' by Greg Williams

'A Practical Guide to Elderly Law – Second Edition' by Justin Patten

'A Practical Guide to Responding to Housing Disrepair and Unfitness Claims' by Iain Wightwick

'A Practical Guide to the Law of Bullying and Harassment in the Workplace' by Philip Hyland

'How to Be a Freelance Solicitor: A Practical Guide to the SRA-Regulated Freelance Solicitor Model' by Paul Bennett

'A Practical Guide to Prison Injury Claims' by Malcolm Johnson

'A Practical Guide to Advising Clients at the Police Station' by Colin Stephen McKeown-Beaumont

'A Practical Guide to Antisocial Behaviour Injunctions – Second Edition' by Iain Wightwick

'Practical Mediation: A Guide for Mediators, Advocates, Advisers, Lawyers, and Students in Civil, Commercial, Business, Property, Workplace, and Employment Cases' by Jonathan Dingle with John Sephton

'The Mini-Pupillage Workbook' by David Boyle

'A Practical Guide to Crofting Law' by Brian Inkster

'A Practical Guide to the Law of Domain Names and Cybersquatting' by Andrew Clemson

'A Practical Guide to the Law of Gender Pay Gap Reporting' by Harini Iyengar

'NHS Whistleblowing and the Law' by Joseph England

'Employment Law and the Gig Economy' by Nigel Mackay & Annie Powell

'A Practical Guide to Noise Induced Hearing Loss (NIHL) Claims' by Andrew Mckie, Ian Skeate, Gareth McAloon

'An Introduction to Beauty Negligence Claims – A Practical Guide for the Personal Injury Practitioner' by Greg Almond

'Intercompany Agreements for Transfer Pricing Compliance' by Paul Sutton

'Zen and the Art of Mediation' by Martin Plowman

'A Practical Guide to Adoption for Family Lawyers' by Graham Pegg

'A Practical Guide to Industrial Disease Claims' by Andrew Mckie & Ian Skeate
'A Practical Guide to Conducting a Sheriff Court Proof' by Andrew Stevenson
'A Practical Guide to Vicarious Liability' by Mariel Irvine
'A Practical Guide to Applications for Landlord's Consent and Variation of Leases' by Mark Shelton
'A Practical Guide to Relief from Sanctions Post-Mitchell and Denton' by Peter Causton
'A Practical Guide to Equity Release for Advisors' by Paul Sams
'A Practical Guide to Financial Services Claims' by Chris Hegarty
'A Practical Guide to Financial Ombudsman Service Claims' by Adam Temple & Robert Scrivenor
'A Practical Guide to Running Housing Disrepair and Cavity Wall Claims – Second Edition' by Andrew Mckie & Ian Skeate
'A Practical Guide to Holiday Sickness Claims – Second Edition' by Andrew Mckie & Ian Skeate
'Arguments and Tactics for Personal Injury and Clinical Negligence Claims' by Dorian Williams
'A Practical Guide to Drone Law' by Rufus Ballaster, Andrew Firman, Eleanor Clot
'On Experts: CPR35 for Lawyers and Experts' by David Boyle
'An Introduction to Personal Injury Law' by David Boyle

www.ingramcontent.com/pod-product-compliance
Lightning Source LLC
LaVergne TN
LVHW022306200926
848481LV00004B/1235
* 9 7 8 1 9 1 6 6 9 8 8 5 7 *